Jonathan and His Birthday Surprises

Story by Coretha Gantling
Illustrations by Coretha and Friends

Published by:

Little Oaks Publishing
www.thepublishedword.com

ISBN: 978-1-964665-11-5

Printed on demand in the U.S., the U.K. and Australia
For Worldwide Distribution

CHAPTER 1

JONATHAN IS TURNING SIX

Jonathan is turning six. Now he is five years young but on Friday November 12, he will have his sixth birthday. He wants to have a party in the zoo.

On Friday, Jonathan wakes up very early. At about 4 AM his eyes open wide, and he stretches out wide in his twin bed. He thinks to himself, "I'm going to look in the mirror and see how I look. I might look different since I am six years old now."

Jonathan remembers that his dad and mom have taught him to pray every morning when he wakes up. So, he get on his knees beside his bed and says:

DEAR FATHER GOD,

THANK YOU FOR PROTECTING ME AS I SLEPT
LAST NIGHT.

THANK YOU, LORD GOD, FOR MY FAMILY,

LORD, KEEP US SAFE EVERY DAY, IN SCHOOL,
AT WORK, AND EVERYWHERE WE GO.

THANK YOU, LORD. AMEN!

CHAPTER 2

JONATHAN LOVES TO TALK TO GOD

After Jonathan prays, he goes into the bathroom and looks in the mirror to see how he looks. He wonders if he has changed since he is now six years old. He looks at his eyes to see if they have changed colors. "No," he says, "my eyes are still the same color as when I was born."

Then Jonathan looks at his ears to see if they have changed. "No," he says, "my ears still look the same size."

Next, he looks at his head and then says, "No, my head looks the same size as before. I'm going to look at my teeth. Maybe I lost my two front teeth like my older sister when she was six. No, I still have all my teeth, even my two front teeth."

"Well," he continues, "I am looking at my hands and my feet, and they still look the same."

"Okay, since everything on me looks the same, I will do my hygiene like my mom taught me to do when I get up. In school, we sing, "This is the way we wash our face, wash our face, wash our face. This is the wash our face so early in the morning."

"This is the way we brush our teeth, brush our teeth, brush our teeth. This is the way we brush our teeth so early in the morning."

"At home, I just brush my teeth."

"Now that I have completed that, I am going to take my bath. I like bubbles in my bath water so I can play and blow bubbles. I put my red boat in the bathtub with me. I love bubble baths. I pretend I am swimming in the ocean."

Jonathan finishes his bath. Next, he puts on his favorite outfit, the one his dad took him to purchase at a children's store in the shopping center near their house.

CHAPTER 3

JONATHAN'S DAY OF SURPRISES

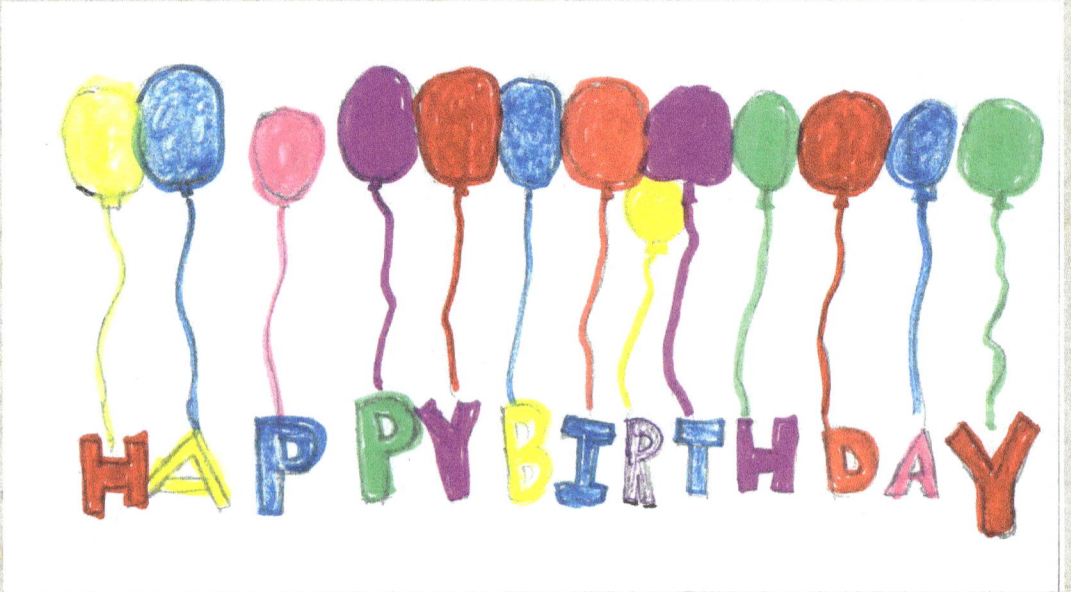

Jonathan is very excited as he begins to get ready for his big day. He thinks to himself, "I can't wait for everyone to wake up and celebrate my birthday with me."

When Jonathan goes downstairs, he finds balloons all over, and each balloon has a number and a message tied to it. He searches for Balloon #1, and when he finds it, he reads the note tied to it. In big, bold, colorful letters like the rainbow, it says,

"HAPPY BIRTHDAY, JONATHAN! WE LOVE YOU!"

Jonathan runs to find Balloon #2 so he can read the note attached to it. When he finds it, he reads, "Jonathan, go into the living room, and you will find a pillow in front of your favorite chair. When you find the pillow, kneel and thank God for your birthday today and praise God for all He has done for you the six years you have been on this earth." Jonathan followed the instructions on the note.

After Jonathan finishes praying, he goes back in the room where he found the balloons to find Balloon #3. He reads the note attached to it. It says, "Look in front of the fireplace, and you will find a surprise."

When Jonathan gets in front of the fireplace, he sees a huge box, and he opens it. Inside the box, he finds six tickets to the zoo, and each ticket has a name on it. The first name is Mark, one of Jonathan's friends. The next ticket says Chris, another friend. The third ticket says Nathan, the next ticket says Anthony, and the last ticket says Jonathan. Each of four of the tickets has the name of one of Jonathan's' friends, and one has his name on it.

Jonathan reads his ticket carefully. It is definitely a ticket to the zoo, exactly where he wanted to go for his birthday. And his friends could go too.

"Balloon time again," thinks Jonathan, so he goes back to find Balloon #4. The message attached to it says, "Go in the kitchen, look on the table, and open the box you will find there." Jonathan finds the box, opens it, and there he finds sunglasses, a blue cap, a pair of blue shorts, and a beautiful shirt with zoo animals all over it. He can see a tiger, a llama, a bear, a zebra, a camel, and a giraffe.

Jonathan runs upstairs to his room and puts his new birthday outfit on. It all fits him perfectly, and he likes it so much.

Jonathan is so excited about all the great surprises he is receiving that he starts singing, "Thank You, Lord, for all You have done for me." He learned that song in his class at church. He almost forgets to go back and find the next balloon to read the note attached to it.

So, now, Jonathan finds Balloon #5. The attached note says, "Knock on Dad and Mom's bedroom door for your next surprise."

Jonathan runs to his parents' room and gently knocks on their door. When he hears his dad say, "Come in, Jonathan," he opens the door and sees his dad and mom with their arms stretched wide to give him birthday hugs. Jonathan notices that his parents have on outfits like his, and there is a box on the bed with his name on it. His mom says, "Jonathan, here is another gift for you." When Jonathan excitedly opens it, he is shocked by what he sees inside. He pulls out two pairs of tennis shoes, the ones he saw and liked when he and his dad went shopping. One pair matches his new outfit, so he takes off his older tennis shoes and puts his new ones on. They fit him perfectly.

Jonathan hugs his parents, thanks them, and then runs to find the last balloon, #6. The message attached to that balloon says, "Go into your sister's room, and you will get another surprise." When Jonathan knocks on his sister's door, she opens it to him, hugs him and then gives him a big box. It's a little heavy, so Jonathan has to put it on the floor.

Just as he is about to open the box, Jonathan hears a funny noise. It sounds like a puppy. He is so happy as he opens the box and finds a puppy just like the one he saw at the pet store the week before when the whole family went there. He picks up his new puppy and cuddles it. The puppy looks up at Jonathan and licks his face.

Jonathan's sister asks, "What are you going to name him?"

He thinks for a few minutes and then says, "I'm going to name him Cuddles."

He takes Cuddles downstairs, and there he sees a puppy bed, food for his puppy, a small crate, and a leash.

Now Jonathan smells food cooking, and he realizes how hungry he is, so he goes into the kitchen where his dad and mom have his birthday breakfast all ready.

After everyone sits down, Jonathan's dad asks him to bless the food, and he does.

His parents have fixed his favorite meal. There are waffles with honey, sausage, scrambled eggs, and orange juice and water.

After breakfast, Jonathan goes back to get his new puppy Cuddles and cuddles him, then puts him on his leash, and together they run to the backyard to play.

" Hi, IAM CUDDLES "

CHAPTER 4

JONATHAN' SIXTH BIRTHDAY ZOO CELEBRATION

Soon Jonathan's parents call him and say, "It's time to go to the zoo." Everyone gets into the family van, they stop and pick up Jonathan's friends, and then head to the zoo.

Jonathan notices that each of his friends has on an outfit exactly like his. He immediately thanks his parents for buying outfits for them all to dress alike for his birthday.

When they arrive at the zoo, they see a big sign that says, "HAPPY BIRTHDAY, JONATHAN!

WELCOME TO THE ZOO!" They all go to the check-in counter and give their tickets to the cashier, who gives them all badges that read, "WELCOME TO JONATHAN'S 6TH BIRTHDAY EXTRAVAGANZA!"

As they go to their assigned area, they find a beautiful set-up with all sorts of large stuffed animals near the table where they will have the birthday party. There is a panda, a giraffe, an elephant, a zebra, and a few other stuffed animals. But Jonathan and his friends are excited to see the real animals, so they set off to find them. They see elephants, tigers, bears, zebras, lions, monkeys, and giraffes. Jonathan likes all of these animals, but he is not very fond of the snakes.

After visiting all the animals in the zoo, they go back to the designated birthday celebration table and have a royal feast. There is all sots of seafood—crab legs, shrimp, fish, and oysters—there is potato salad, finger sandwiches, po boy sandwiches, and plenty of fruit. They even eat watermelon and cantaloupe cut in the shape of zoo animals. They also enjoy strawberries, plumbs, peaches, cherries, and more.

And you should see Jonathan's birthday cake. It is in the shape of his favorite animal, a dog, and on the front of it is a photo of him with his new puppy, Cuddles.

Jonathan has so much fun at his sixth birthday celebration. Maybe you can come to his sixteenth birthday celebration ... or even sooner. Don't tell his parents, but when he blew out the six candles on his birthday cake, he wished for a family-and-friends cruise for his tenth birthday.

www.ingramcontent.com/pod-product-compliance
Lightning Source LLC
LaVergne TN
LVHW081328060426
835513LV00012B/1239